INTERVENTION
SET
SELECTION

SIMONE G. SYMONETTE

authorHOUSE®

AuthorHouse™
1663 Liberty Drive
Bloomington, IN 47403
www.authorhouse.com
Phone: 833-262-8899

Published by AuthorHouse 09/01/2022

ISBN: 978-1-6655-6860-9 (sc)
ISBN: 978-1-6655-6858-6 (hc)
ISBN: 978-1-6655-6859-3 (e)

Library of Congress Control Number: 2022915301

Print information available on the last page.

This book is printed on acid-free paper.

CONTENTS

LIST OF FIGURES

AN ANALOGY

How a consultant selects an intervention set is similar to how a physician selects a treatment. If a patient complains to their physician about a health issue, such as pain in their stomach, it is very rare that the physician will prescribe a single medicine to address the problem without subsequent analysis of the patient's condition. The initial patient analysis consists of the physician making observations and asking questions in order to arrive at a treatment based on the evaluation of the patient's conditions. This is similar to what a performance improvement consultant refers to as the analysis phase and is typically done with the aid of diagnostic and process models.

Analysis and intervention set selection work in tandem to power the final intervention set the practitioner selects, designs, develops, and implements. Just as a physician selects a course of treatment based on a prior experience, a consultant's analysis informs his or her intervention set selection. The two processes converge when a consultant's analysis questions leads the consultant to check and confirm their assumptions about a particular performance problem. This is referred to as comprehension of the situations and leads the way for the second and third components.

Similar to the physician illustration, as the consultant asks more questions, they also draw upon their prior experiences; that is, a cluster of interventions or problems they have encountered in the past. Drawing upon previous experiences activates the various schemata. The schemata continuously change as a consultant answers new questions about the performance problem, allowing the intervention set to take shape. Returning to the example, the consultant also seeks guidance or advice from other sources just as a medical doctor may turn to physician's reference books or electronic database references. For the performance consultant, these references may also come in the form of books on interventions and classification of models as well as journal articles and case studies. If a treatment is not selected after referring to the literature, the physician may then contact other experts and colleagues in their network who are familiar with other specific cases of the problem and can provide insights into how to proceed with diagnosing and selecting a treatment. While this is taking place, the consultant's schemata are changing as they accommodate and assimilate the new information to further comprehend the situation and select an intervention set. In turn, this engages the second component of the substantive theory of intervention set selection: activating schemata to synthesize an intervention set.

Reasoning is necessary for a consultant to adjust and to accommodate the contextual intricacies of each performance problem. Similar to rare illness cases, the treatments are not straight forward. A patient's treatment may be experimental, regimented, and conducted over a period of time and requiring follow-up visits for further observation. When prescribing a medicine, a medical doctor may emphasize the need for other treatment recommendations such as adequate rest, exercise, and increased water intake since they may aid in the effectiveness of the prescribed medicine. Similarly, throughout the intervention set selection process, a consultant needs to adhere to governing principles when making their recommendations, so their intervention sets are properly implemented and most effective in solving the performance gap. This book's principles serve in the same capacity as the principles physicians should follow when recommending treatments to patients.

The Role of Reasoning

The reasoning skills a consultant uses to select an intervention set is similar to the approach a physician uses when selecting a patient's treatment.

The act of thinking in order to put together seemingly disconnected interventions is at the heart of intervention set selection. The ideas presented in this book force consultants to enhance their reasoning skills. Deductive reasoning allows a consultant to apply known outcomes to specific performance problems in the form of heuristics and other forms of tested problem solving. Although deductive reasoning is essential to the process, it may become limiting, especially in complex performance improvement situations. While performance problems have similarities, the context of each organization's performance problem is unique. The details of each case faced in the field requires the consultant to also engage in inductive reasoning to select intervention sets. Acquiring and refining inductive reasoning skills is advantageous for experienced consultants since they encounter more complex performance problems in the field. However, it is the abductive reasoning or conjecture thinking that tends to be the most difficult to develop because it involves creativity and intuition. The schemata, principles, and modelling techniques presented in this book should be used to facilitate this type of reasoning. The honing of reasoning skills through practice is what sets an expert apart from a novice. Experience also helps a consultant maintain confidence when faced with limited information.

Profit, not-for profit, and government organizations all have one thing in common, the need to improve performance at the worker, process, and organization levels. Understanding what combination of interventions will influence behaviors in a desired direction and improve performance is not simple, nor is it easily understood by researchers or practitioners in the field of human performance improvement (Langdon, Whiteside, & McKenna, 1999). An intervention is defined as "a course of action taken to improve performance. It is planned and purposeful, and requires organizations and the people in them to behave differently" (Pershing, 2006, p.12).

Langdon, Whiteside, and McKenna (1999) suggest that gaps in performance can be reduced or closed through the proper selection of interventions. This distinctive problem-solving approach revolves around key attributes a consult should aspire to; these include the ability to select interventions that are results-oriented, cost-effective, comprehensive, and systemic (Pershing, 2006; Spitzer, 1992).

Although scholars mention the idea of combinations or multiple interventions, there is limited evidence to support this idea. Also, many organizations often only prescribe one intervention, training, as a remedy to address performance. In order to add to the understanding of practitioners, this book focuses on how consultants select multiple interventions that work together to close or reduce performance problems. The goal here is to offer an approach to "thinking" and "doing" as individuals engage in intervention set selection. The intend is to help consultants in their everyday work but also to spark inspiration, generate ideas, and take this topic beyond the foundations presented. Knowing how to appropriately choose a course of action or intervention requires an understanding of how theory explains the possible outcomes of multiple performance factors working in unison. Understanding the theory behind why an intervention should be selected not only reduces the possibility of unexpected results, but also allows an individual to better explain why a course of action should be taken from a theoretical perspective that can be tested. This book is a response to the gaps in the literature of human performance improvement related to intervention selection. The following questions will be answered throughout this text:

- How do practicing professionals select interventions?
- Are there discernible patterns that practicing professionals follow when selecting interventions?
- Are there principles that guide intervention selection?
- Are there elements involved in designing interventions that are schematic?
- What is the underlying theory or model that explains intervention selection, including specific relationships between performance factors? What is the theory and does it inform intervention selection?

The result of this exploration is significant because it 1) focuses on the development of theory, 2) sets a foundation for future inquiry, 3) provides a guide for the practical application of models and principles, and 4) unearthing a method to which consultants may adhere in order to demonstrate the value of their knowledge and expertise.

Implications for Future Research

By introducing new principles, schemata, and a substantive theory for intervention set selection, this book expands the performance improvement field. The findings compel educators, practitioners, and scholars to rethink how performance improvement is taught, studied, and applied, especially the methods and practices of intervention set selection. Instead of skimming over the "how" and "why" of intervention set selection between the analysis phase to the design phase, this work refocuses the literature on the key component of intervention set selection. The significance of this text rests in the development of a substantive theory and the foundation it lays for future scientific inquiry and formal theory development. It also has practical and career implications for consultants to consider when engaging in performance improvement and honing their intervention set selection skills. Since each industry has its own distinctions, a consultant should specialize in a particular industry such as education, manufacturing, or healthcare in order to bring added value to clients. As a prerequisite, consultants also should have a strong foundational knowledge and years of practical application in the performance improvement field. It also suggests that novice, mid-career, and expert consultants all must make continuous efforts to stay current with new research and practices. Finally, these concepts should enable practitioners to better articulate the value of their work to organizations, which is not only a valuable skill but also a necessity for the field.

Scholarly Foundation

This book is based on Symonette (2015), a dissertation titled "Developing Principles and Schemata for Intervention Set Selection in Human Performance Technology". The dissertation's literature review provides an examination of the lack of knowledge on factors that influence intervention selection specific to systemic thinking and diffusion of effect. Noting that the literature also only provides a narrow explanation of the role that models can play in the intervention selection process. The dissertation explains that the limited number of principles guiding intervention selection that are available to practitioners needs to be expanded. It highlights the absence of research focused on the theoretical understanding of intervention selection a void that this book seeks to fill. As well as adds to the literature on how professionals select intervention, specifically with regard to what is involved in the selection process. This is done in the dissertation by providing empirical evidence demonstrating how performance improvement professionals tend to select interventions and offers principles designed to guide a practitioner through the intervention selection process. Finally, it provides some understanding about the relationship between performance factors within a group of interventions.

The methods chapter of the dissertation provides an explanation of grounded theory as defined by its originating authors, Glaser and Strauss (1967) in detail. It also identifies how the two authors differ in terms of applying the method and explains the approach utilized in the dissertation. The role of the researcher is examined, along with a practical explanation of grounded theory. The dissertation provides an overview of grounded theory's application in the original study. This includes an explanation of how the data sources were identified and sampled as well as a description of case selection criteria. Also, included are illustrations of the theoretical sampling process which highlights the iterative process of collecting data, code creation, and the analysis of data. Explanations of open coding procedures, the extensive use of memos, the emergence of a core category, and the creation of models to enable theoretical scheme or substantive theory. The methods chapter of the dissertation concludes with an explanation of the critical elements that emerged to form the scheme. This book presents the findings of Symonette's (2015) work in a more business friendly manner so that the principles and schemata may be used by a business audience. Readers may find it helpful to review the literature review and methods founded in the original dissertation to gain more insights into the text presented here.

INITIATING PRINCIPLES

Initiating Principle 1: Client's attention

> *Client's attention. A performance consultant should demonstrate how the performance problem aligns with strategic goals. Establishing a connection between strategic goals and performance problems provides the consultant with an opportunity to gain and maintain the client's attention throughout the life of the project and builds creditability.*

Whether internal or external to the organization, a trigger or symptom forced the stakeholders to pay attention to the performance because it could threaten the organization's survival or be an opportunity for growth and expansion. Early in the process the consultant engages in a client learning process or relationship building that is a part of the overall analysis process.

This relationship is also essential to the intervention selection process and ensures that the lines of communication remain open throughout the project. The concept of learning about the client is documented in the performance improvement literature (Rush, 2012). More research on how to leverage the client's learning informational process for value added consultation, including client home remedy behavior, triggers, symptoms, and attention grabbers is needed in the literature.

This client learning process involves the consultant identifying the triggers, symptoms, and attention grabbers so that they can understand the organization's history, motives, actions taken, environment, and data. Triggers, symptoms, and attention grabbers are items that help the consultant to articulate client criteria for intervention design and selection. Client criteria are often implicitly stated through the initial description of the problem and allow practitioners to understand what will satisfy the client needs at the most general level. It also helps them to communicate in the organization's language. Triggers, symptoms, and attention grabber findings helped to deduce several principles that focus on client criteria for closing the performance gap. This initiating principle is necessary for the performance consultant to adhere to when building and maintaining a client relationship. A performance consultant should:

- Gain an understanding of the organizational situation through the eyes of the client. This perspective can provide valuable data points that serve as client criteria for the performance improvement initiative.

- Identify what gets the client's attention and what is a trigger for the client to take action.

- Learn and use the organization's language throughout the client learning process and in identifying the performance problem. Using a common language throughout the performance improvement process allows the client to understand the value added by the consultation.

- Study the symptoms and what they are tangibly connected to inside and outside the organization and use this as a focal point for data collection.

Initiating Principle 2: Client self-diagnoses

> *Client self-diagnoses and home remedy. A performance consultant should inquire about any prior self-diagnosis activity conducted by the client to address the performance problem. In addition to analyzing the performance problem, be ready to evaluate any home remedies initiated by the client.*

Knowing what motivates the organization to take action to address a performance problem in the midst of other business needs is an essential task.

Understanding how an organization self-diagnoses and attempts to treat a performance problem is important information for the performance consultant to know. Self-diagnoses and intervention actions can be the cause of additional problems that may need to be addressed. Prior to consultation and analysis by a performance consultant, some stakeholders may conduct some form of self-diagnosing regarding the performance problem.

Before diving into the selection of an intervention set one needs to seek out prior information on the client's involvement in addressing the problem. The point at which the behavior patterns of a client and a professional tend to merge, is when an organizational trigger or symptom becomes too complex for a home remedy solution. Understanding the *home remedy* behavior a client takes before a professional becomes involved helps the professional diagnosis the performance problem and any additional problems that the home remedy may have caused. The four key home remedy patterns identified include:

1. Seeking a method for solving a problem without understanding problems
2. Degree of change or lack of collaboration
3. Greater attention makes the client more aware of problem areas without specificity
4. Formulation of preconceived solutions to address problem areas

As a principle, a performance consultant should investigate any self-diagnoses and homemade remedies implemented by the organization during the initial relationship building and client learning process. Adherence to this initiating principle helps the practitioner to use what was done as an advantage instead of a hindrance. A performance consultant should:

- Identify any adverse events that resulted from client home remedies and ensure interventions are selected to address the additional problem.
- Build on any positive results of home remedies. Building on successful outcomes helps to create buy-in, limits redundant efforts, and helps to make the client initiative seem continuous to the end user.

Initiating Principle 3: Analysis and tacit knowledge

Analysis and tacit knowledge work together. A consultant must appropriately and wisely balance the use of data resulting from analysis and tacit knowledge as they navigate the intervention set selection phase of the performance improvement process. The two types of knowledge should not be viewed as dichotomies, but as counterparts working together to energize the intervention set selection phase.

The principle that data drives the selection of an intervention is not a new concept in the literature on performance improvement. This text challenges the idea that data analysis automatically reveals what groups of interventions to select as suggested by predominant models in the field. It is critical that data collection tools and data analysis results be interpreted by a practitioner well versed in the performance literature, specifically in the case of multiple interventions being selected to address performance problems, because analysis provides answers to specific questions but not how to connect the answers to a comprehensive group of interventions. In general, the practitioner should continuously refresh and seek new literature on performance improvement research, theories, and case studies in order to expand their knowledge of the performance landscape and to make a meaningful interpretation and use of the data gathered. Adherence to this initiating principle will help the practitioner to achieve a comprehensive approach to intervention selection.

- Stay abreast of new and old diagnostic and process models.

- Regardless if practitioners are using extant data or data they collected, a comparison of interventions that result from the analysis against all the performance factors is required; that is connect the dots.

- Make an illustration of the connections in model form.

- Identify how each individual intervention reinforce one another and ascertain if there were any interventions that were overlooked in the analysis process that would assist with reducing the performance gap. If the data collection was inadequate it is likely that the analysis may not yield enough information to reduce the performance gap.

- Performance improvement professionals should use their tacit knowledge of the literature base and experience to add value. That is, provide insight from the theoretical level not observed in the current data set but founded in the literature base of the discipline.

There are patterns a consultant tend to follow when selecting interventions. Although patterns may take place before any actual intervention is selected, they are critical to the intervention selection decision making process. These patterns explain how the practitioner begins to learn about the client, how the client tried to address the problem with homemade remedies and data analysis results; all of which later aid the scoping process and inform the intervention selection decision making process.

The fourth initiating principle is divided into two parts. 4a focuses on the role of a consultant as an interconnected entity within the organization and the performance improvement process. While 4b focuses on the cross-functional nature of a consultant in the intervention set selection process. Both principles have similar characteristics but are distinct enough to be presented as unique principles.

Initiating Principle 4a: Interconnectedness

Interconnectedness. A consultant should act as an orchestra leader. To do this the consultant must be interconnected to people, networks, and ideas within and outside of the client organization. Consultant interconnectedness goes beyond general knowledge and awareness of these entities. Consultants should immerse themselves into these environments in order to assure that the selected intervention set ultimately fits into the current and evolving new environment. If the consultant is not interconnected they can potentially select an intervention set that quickly becomes obsolete because it does not fit within the environment.

No intervention is an island. Interventions are connected and very rarely does an intervention stand on its own to reduce a performance gap (Pershing, 2006). It would be similar to building a bridge with only a pile of wood and nails without blueprints, or a team of workers. As a principle it is the practitioner's responsibility:

- to be knowledgeable about how performance factors are connected by being well grounded in multiple disciplines.
- to identify connections between interventions and the characteristics of each relationship.

Initiating Principle 4b: Seek cross-functionality

Seek internal and external cross-functionality. A consultant must work across disciplines, departments, and industries to select an intervention set that is comprehensive. Cross-functionality allows an intervention set to generate support and buy-in utilizing the knowledge base from other disciplines so that the set gains traction within the organization. Cross-functionality means more than just having the right people in the room and a diverse set of ideas on the table. It involves a deeper understanding of how cross –functional intervention sets impact performance. It requires conscious and deliberate connections between ideas and people. The consultant should be viewed as a creditable connector and selector of intervention sets that need to be implemented.

A consultant must work across disciplines, departments, and industries to select an intervention set that is comprehensive. Cross-functionality allows the intervention set to generate support and buy-in from the knowledge base of other disciplines so that the set gains traction within the organization. Initiating principle 4b builds on other principles in that it requires the consultant to now focus on a range and span of control of the intervention set versus the depth and expertise required in previous principles. A consultant should be willing and able to venture outside of their comfort interventions to explore possibilities.

A consultant adds value to a project in several ways by implementing the cross functionality principle. First, cross-functionality deeply ingrains the intervention set into the organization, reduces redundancy, diminishes misalignment at the strategic level, and allows the implementation of the intervention set to be more easily adopted by an organization that operates in silos. The principle of cross-functionality requires the consultant to:

- stay abreast of the latest research and best practices in a variety of areas;
- maintain an extended network inside and outside the field of performance improvement;
- maintain a sense of curiosity to make connections on a theoretical bases in a variety of areas;

- transfer theoretical understanding from one area or function to another to address the problem at hand; and

- communicate across multiple disciples, industries, departments, and so on.

The theoretical foundation of the field also alludes to the idea of a combination of interventions; however, it provides limited explanation of how and why interventions work as a set. Systems and field theory present some insight on the idea that a combination of interventions is needed to address performance gaps; however, no information is provided on how combinations of interventions are selected and for what reasons. Therefore, a more appropriate word is needed to meet this void in the literature that accounts for the integrated and connected nature of interventions as a *set* or the term *intervention set*. Referring to more than one intervention working together as a set is more appropriate than simply changing the word intervention into its plural form interventions because it takes into consideration how each intervention within the set works in coordination with others to bridge performance gaps. The word *set* has several meanings, however, both the noun and verb form of set are compatible with the human performance technology (HPT) literature. As a verb, *set* means:

…to place in some relation to something or someone: *We set a supervisor over the new workers*…to adjust (a mechanism) so as to control its performance…to fix at a given point or calibration…to cause to take a particular direction. (Dictionary. com online dictionary, 2010)

As a noun, *set* is referred to as:

…a collection of articles designed for use together: *a set of china; a chess set*…A collection, each member of which is adapted for special use in a particular operation: *a set of golf clubs; a set of carving knives*. (Dictionary.com online dictionary, 2010)

As noted, in seeking a more precise word or term to explain the relationship between various interventions that are intentionally selected to bring about a change in performance, this study uses the term *intervention set*. It adequately describes the collection of interventions used as a cohesive whole to address performance gaps. Now that the definitions of an intervention set has been examined, it is necessary to turn attention to refining how intervention sets are selected and why, so that the voids in the literature about the process of intervention selection can be reduced.

Prerequisite Principle 1: Acquire practical experience

Acquire practical experience. Novice consultants should begin by practicing on small performance improvement projects and by reading the work of more seasoned professionals in order to start acquiring foundational schemata. The combination of education and real world practice can vary; however, the goal is for the consultant to be well grounded in both applied research and practice. After a consultant has many years of experience and an advance degree in performance improvement, they must stay abreast of new research and additions to best practices as well as actively engage in professional associations. This is important so that experienced individuals do not become stuck in the habit of operating without incorporating new and improved methods, which in turn can render their practice stagnant.

Novice consultants should begin by practicing on small performance improvement projects and by reading the work of more seasoned professionals in the field in order to start acquiring foundational schemata. Once they have some practical experience, they should seek certification to validate their ability to conduct performance improvement. In his book, *Outliers* (2011), Malcolm Gladwell argues that to be considered an expert, an individual must dedicate years of practice to refining their craft. Gladwell's idea of dedicated practice over time is known as the 10,000 hour rule and refers to an individual acquiring at least 10,000 hours of correct practice on a particular skill. A consultant can acquire performance improvement experience and practice in a variety of ways. For example, a consultant can acquire experience through pursuing a graduate degree focused on performance improvement and then spend seven to eight years in the industry refining their practice. Or an individual might pursue a PhD in the area of performance for four to seven years and then spend three to six years practicing in industry. The combination of education and real world practice can vary; however, the goal is for the consultant to be well grounded in both research and practice.

This principle also maintains that even after a consultant has many years of experience and an advance degree in performance they must stay abreast of new research and additions to best practices as well as actively engage in professional associations. This is important so that experienced individuals do not stuck in the habit of operating without incorporating new and improved methods, which in turn can render their practice stagnant.

Prerequisite Principle 2: Acquire expertise and collaboration

Acquire expertise and when lacking seek collaboration. A performance consultant must acquire subject matter expertise in at least one phase of the performance improvement process. The consultant should be honest with themselves and the client about their skill level. When the consultant lacks needed expertise they should collaborate with an expert to supplement the lacking skill required for the intervention set to be executed in the organization.

Collaboration and subject matter expertise are presented as a part of the same principle because consultants should rely on partnerships in situations in which they are not experts. This allows them to draw upon others' strengths to identify and achieve desired results. It is nearly impossible to have a deep expertise in all aspects of performance interventions (Van Tiem, Mosely & Dessinger, 2004; Spitzer 1999). While organizing and project management are core skills a consultant must possess, a consultant must be grounded in all aspects of the performance improvement process, such as analysis, design, development, implementation, and evaluation.

The more expertise consultants can acquire, the more it enables them to see the intricacies of the systems into which the intervention set will be implemented. Having deep expertise expands the selection options available to the consultant and enables them to see further into the possibility of the intervention set because it widens their ability to see systemically. Perfecting a specific niche area where there is limited expertise enables the consultant to add value. A consultant should also have deep expertise in a particular industry or culture as well as a few interventions they have mastered. If subject matter expertise is not acquired, the consultant runs the risk of simply taking orders from the client, which diminishes the value they bring to reducing the performance gap. As suggested by Pershing (2006) the performance consultant should serve as an orchestra leader who organizes the many moving components but be able to focus attention on particular parts of the process if there is a problem.

Collaboration allows for consultants to identify and engage the right individuals in the project at hand. It also helps specific individuals to focus on their area of expertise. More importantly, collaboration offers the consulting team an interpreter to guide them through the organizational nomenclature and structures.

Defining Intervention Set Selection

Intervention set selection is the process of strategically choosing a group of purposeful actions that address a related performance factor deficiency. Each intervention within the set works complementary to the other to reduce or close performance gaps. The process occurs after the initial performance analyses phase and takes place in tandem with the design and development phases of the performance improvement process. The process involves manipulating each intervention within a given set so that each is calibrated with others in order to obtain optimum performance and to build the power of the set as a cohesive unit. The selection of intervention sets can include the selection of multiple smaller intervention sets to make-up a more complex set. The quality of the final selected intervention set is dependent on time and the skill of the consultant. As suggested by the performance improvement design and development literature, calibration is achieved through a series of rapid prototyping cycles (Wedman & Tessmer, 1990). Complete equilibrium and finality is rarely achieved because of time constraints and varying skills of the consultant. As a result, a consultant should communicate intervention set selection in terms of reducing a performance gap versus completely closing it. This definition argues that, regardless of size, it is the most effective and efficient combination of interventions that can maintain equilibrium within a system that is the most desirable.

The performance factors mentioned in this definition comes from the factors outlined in Wile's (1996) work, which include: organizational systems, incentives, cognitive support, tools, knowledge and skill, physical environment, and inherent ability. This definition of intervention set selection is informed by both general systemic thinking and diffusion of effect. To explain the process of intervention set selection in its entirety and to provide a foundation for a substantive theory, intervention set schemata are provided.

CHAPTER 3

SCHEMATA ELEMENTS OF INTERVENTION SET SELECTION

The field of performance improvement has numerous process and diagnostic models that provide how-to-knowledge in identifying critical concepts and procedural tasks. These models enable practitioners, typically novices, to apply these core concepts and tasks in the field. This book takes consultants' experiences that have become automatic and presents them as schemata to explain how this approach to thinking about intervention selection is central to the intervention set selection process. Six different schemata for intervention sets with individual guiding principles are presented and used to shed light on the intervention set selection process undertaken by performance consultants.

Composition schemata

The composition schema is the first and most essential of the intervention set schema. The composition schema refers to how many interventions are involved in closing a performance gap. That is whether there is an intervention set or a single intervention. See Figure 1. It is possible, although rare, that a single intervention can close a performance gap; however, knowing and being able to recall the composition schemata is the first cognitive structure that a consultant must identify in the selection process. A single intervention can be simply introducing a new organizational goal. However, simply developing goals will not be all that is needed for those goals to be realized.

Single Intervention	Intervention Set

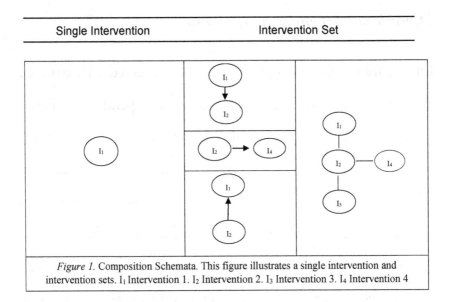

Figure 1. Composition Schemata. This figure illustrates a single intervention and intervention sets. I_1 Intervention 1. I_2 Intervention 2. I_3 Intervention 3. I_4 Intervention 4

Figure 1: Composition Schemata

By drawing on a composition schemata and a systems mindset a consultant is prompted to think differently about interventions, even if the analysis reveals that an organization lacks goals. Composition schemata can be visualized in a number of combinations with varying performance contexts. This multitude of possibilities generated further intervention set schemata as well as permeating interventions set schemata principles that are discussed in chapter 4.

Directional dependence schemata

Interventions are not optimized when selected in isolation. Similar to the composition schema is the dependence schema which explains the linkage and direction between interventions within a set. As show in Figure 2, the directional dependence schema provides the consultants with depth and direction when systemically thinking about an intervention set. Intervention sets with depth provide a more stable approach to performance improvement because they are supported by other interventions that impact the performance factors. The directional aspect of this schema helps to think about other possible performance factors that may be at play. While this may seem logical, the concept can elude a novice resulting in an ill structured intervention set.

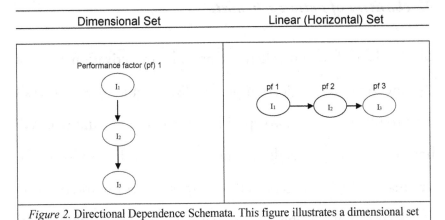

Figure 2. Directional Dependence Schemata. This figure illustrates a dimensional set and linear (horizontal) set. I_1 Intervention 1. I_2 Intervention 2. I_3 Intervention 3. pf 1 Performance factor 1. pf 2 Performance factor 2. pf 3 Performance factor 3.

Figure 2: Directional Dependence Schema

A directional dependence schema is a dimensional view of intervention sets, meaning that one intervention within the same performance factor category may need other lower order interventions within the same performance factor to tighten the performance gap closure. The schema can be linear or horizontal, meaning that the interventions within the intervention set can cut across performance factors but still need each other to reduce the performance gap. A training intervention is dependent on a higher order intervention within a performance factor such as an organizational goal, new procedure, or new program. Therefore, intervention sets have dependent relationships within the set with one high order intervention that begins the dependence chain.

Mechanism of action schemata

Mechanism of action schemata provide an activation view of the intervention set selection process (See Figure 3). An analysis may result in one or two specific interventions being selected; however, a skilled consultant relies on their mechanism of action schemata to fill in the gaps in the analysis to form an intervention set. A consultant is able to use their experience and theoretical understanding of given interventions to see the connections between interventions that are not visible from the analysis alone. One intervention can activate the need for two or three interventions that were not directly identifiable from the analysis.

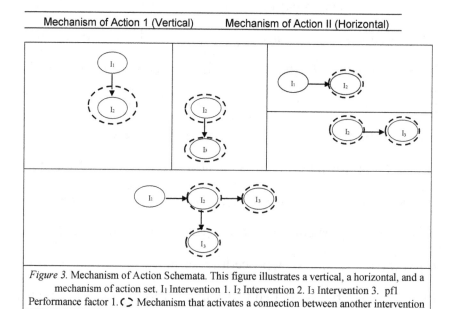

Mechanism of Action 1 (Vertical)   Mechanism of Action II (Horizontal)

Figure 3. Mechanism of Action Schemata. This figure illustrates a vertical, a horizontal, and a mechanism of action set. I₁ Intervention 1. I₂ Intervention 2. I₃ Intervention 3. pfl Performance factor 1. ⊂⊃ Mechanism that activates a connection between another intervention

Figure 3: Mechanism of Action Schemata

Enforcement schemata

Enforcement schemata allow the consultant to quickly see what interventions are susceptible to failing if selected in isolation. A skilled consultant would be able to decide if a single intervention is vulnerable and needs reinforcement from another intervention within the same performance factor category or another. Enforcement schemata build on the dependence aspect of the directional dependence schemata previously mentioned, but they are different in that the enforcement schemata can be one-way or two-way directional; that is cyclical. See Figure 4. When interventions in a set reinforce one another, the set is a tighter combined force.

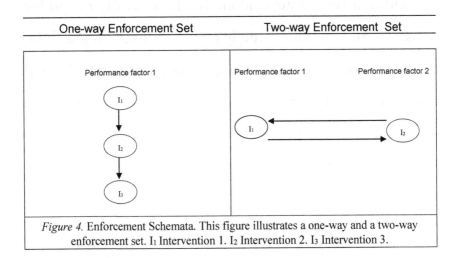

Figure 4. Enforcement Schemata. This figure illustrates a one-way and a two-way enforcement set. I_1 Intervention 1. I_2 Intervention 2. I_3 Intervention 3.

Figure 4: Enforcement Schemata

Transformation schemata

The transformation schemata are readily accessible concepts stored in the consultant's memory that informs them that some interventions have a greater impact or trickledown effect than others. See Figure 5. Some interventions carry more weight in an intervention set because they fall under a more predominant performance factor such as organizational systems. Gilmore (2009) referred to this more powerful intervention as the primary intervention. For the purposes of examining intervention set selection they will be referred to as higher, medium, and low transformational power interventions because an intervention set can come in a variety of sequences with sub intervention sets within a larger intervention. The high, medium, and low transformation schemata simply give the consultant the ability to quickly see the transformative impact an intervention will have on others in a set.

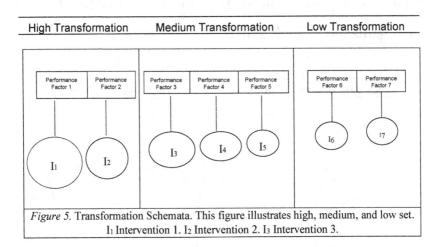

Figure 5. Transformation Schemata. This figure illustrates high, medium, and low set. I_1 Intervention 1. I_2 Intervention 2. I_3 Intervention 3.

Figure 5: Transformation Schemata

Reverberation schemata

Reverberation schemata are a way for consultants to quickly think about the impact the intervention set implementation will have on the organization. Diagramming the connections between interventions as noted in the mechanism of action schemata helps to identify the impact more easily. An intervention set's impact can be narrow in scope and impact a particular part of the organization. See Figure 6.

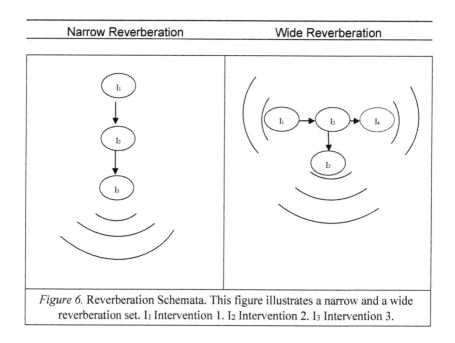

Figure 6. Reverberation Schemata. This figure illustrates a narrow and a wide reverberation set. I_1 Intervention 1. I_2 Intervention 2. I_3 Intervention 3.

Figure 6: Reverberation Schemata

Wide reverberation schemata refer to larger intervention sets that are broader in scope and influence multiple functions in the organization. These schemata reflect the structural thought process consultants take when thinking through how to select an intervention set. Schemata build off each other to illustrate the elements of intervention set selection and illustrate mental structures used to select intervention sets. A performance consultant activates schemata stored in memory that allows them to quickly retrieve knowledge about past experiences when there are missing data or if an analysis is not robust and is done before their involvement in the project. This is one of the reasons skilled consultants can sense that a single intervention is most often not the only intervention needed in most instances. In instances where performance analysis is lacking, the consultant fills in gaps or slots in the analysis with knowledge from previous experiences then seeks to confirm their hypothesis without having to conduct another formal analysis. If a novice only relies on the one-to-one match of performance to intervention based on the results of an analysis, they would be missing the power of an intervention set. This approach to intervention selection is often a result of simply relaying on models and heuristics to inform the selection of interventions without consideration of the art, science, and intuition aspect of the intervention set selection process. Knowing how to use performance models and heuristics is a prerequisite to understanding what is necessary for the initial problem and intervention identification. However, these models and heuristics become limiting when focusing on the intervention set selection process. That is why the schemata and principles presented here become more valuable in instances of new performance problems for more skilled practitioners.

PERMEATING PRINCIPLES

***Permeating Principle 1a: Intervention
set system perspective***

> *Intervention set systems perspective. A systems
> mindset needs to permeate the intervention set
> selection process. The consultant should pay special
> attention on what binds each intervention together
> as a set, how the complete set works together as
> one unified set, and how the set functions within
> an organization. A systems mindset during the
> intervention set selection process allows the analysis
> to be optimized through the use of schemata.*

As a principle a consultant should take a systems perspective
to identify whether the performance gap requires a single
intervention or a set of interventions to reduce the performance

gap. An analysis may result in a single intervention as the root cause of the performance problem, but the composition schema helps the consultant to see the system that revolves around that single intervention and to make a determination if the performance problem requires a single versus a set of interventions. The composition schema is useful because the analysis informing the intervention selection process may not have been conducted by the consultant and may not have been thoroughly completed. Analysis questions are critical to the intervention selection process because they frame the thinking about the possibilities of intervention. If the analysis is done haphazardly or by a novice it can have a limiting effect on the comprehensiveness of the intervention set selected (Pershing, 2006). A systems mindset should guide the decision to choose a single versus a set of interventions. A systems view requires the consultant to focus on the arrangement of properties within a system and now these properties work together as a whole (Bertalanffy, 1972; Brethower, 1999; Rosenberg, 1999; Girard, Lapides & Roe, 2006). Systems thinking tends to fall into the performance literature that is focused on the performance problem analysis; however, this text contends that system thinking is essential to the intervention selection process and is done unconsciously by expert consultants when analyses are lacking. Thinking with a systems perspective expands a consultant's view of the possible interconnectedness of interventions to reduce a performance gap. The implementation of systems thinking during the intervention set selection process allows the analysis to be optimized.

Permeating Principle 1b: Consider consequence and reflect

> *Consider the consequence of each intervention and reflect on the intervention set. Consultants should always consider the consequences of each intervention selected as a part of an intervention set. In doing so, the consultant should look at all the interventions in the set as a whole to identify how they work together and what keeps them functioning cohesively. A consultant may not know all the consequences of the set with certainty, but a good faith effort should be taken to gain knowledge about potential risks.*

Consultants should always consider the consequences of each intervention they select as a part of an intervention set. In doing so, the consultant should look at all the interventions in the set as a whole to identify how they work together and what keeps them functioning cohesively. This principle is based on Gilbert's (1978/2007) idea of diffusion of effect where no single intervention should have a maximizing effect but its function should generate power for the other interventions in the set (Chyunh, 2005). No one single intervention should carry so much weight that it could stand by itself without other supporting interventions that work in a combined set to reduce the performance gap.

Permeating Principle 1c: Understand the impact of the set

> *Understand the impact of the set. It is the responsibility of the performance consultant to inform the client of the intentional or unintentional impact the selected intervention set may have on other parts of the organization and surrounding community. This allows the client to prepare and keeps the client consultant relationship healthy.*

Occasionally stepping back and focusing on the intervention set as a system that will be implemented into a larger organization system is important. Without doing so, the consultant is not able to install safeguards for a healthy implementation of the set. Knowing the impact the set will have on the organization also allows the consultant to prepare the client for what to expect as a result of the implementation. Keeping the client aware of the possible impact to other parts of the organization or the industry as whole is essential to a healthy partnership.

Permeating Principle 2: Select an evidence-based set

Select an evidence-based intervention set. A consultant must move beyond only gathering evidence during the needs analysis phase and gather evidence on individual interventions and sets of interventions. This evidence should be sought through a deep understanding of performance improvement published research and theory as well as through evidence acquired during practical experience and observation in the field.

An evidence-based approach to performance improvement is a hallmark of the field; however, experts in the field have criticized practitioners for the lack of theoretical and research implementation when it comes to suggesting solutions to performance problem (Stolovitch, 2000; Clark and Estes, 2000). Due to many years of experience in an area, expert consultant's concept of theory can often simply be based on that experience rather than any validation by an outside entity. A performance consultant should have a deep understanding of how to use research and theory to complete a comprehensive analysis, but also how to use those same skills when selecting an intervention set and taking the process one step further by citing evidence or theory supporting their selected intervention set. By having a vast and deep understanding of performance research and theory, a consultant is better equipped to serve the client and select an intervention set that is based on evidence. Evidence based intervention set principles can be determined through the first-hand experience of consultants or through established and well-researched theory.

The third permeating principle is divided into two parts because there are elements of principles demanding specific attention and guidance for performance consultants. 3a focuses on the balancing act between art, science, and intuition that performance consultants must constantly maintain in the intervention set selection process. While permeating principle 3b guards against using template or cookie cutter approaches to intervention set selection.

Permeating Principle 3a: Balance art, science, and intuition

> *Balance art, science, and intuition. A consultant's intuition and artistic expression should not be ignored in the quest for scientific reasoning nor should it be the sole basis for the selection of an intervention set. Intuition and artistic expression need to be done in tandem within a scientific process and grounded in evidence-based practices.*

Consultants should consistently keep in mind that there are elements of art, science, and intuition to the process of intervention set selection. Selecting an intervention set based on scientific reasoning is specifically highlighted in another principle of this study: Select an evidence-based intervention set. However, a consultant's intuition and artistic expression should not be ignored in the quest for scientific reasoning nor should it be the sole basis for the selection of an intervention set. Intuition and artistic expression needs to be done in tandem with a scientific process and evidence based rationale.

Permeating Principle 3b: Avoid the cookie cutter approach

> *Avoid the cookie cutter approach. A cookie cutter approach refers to a consultant promoting an intervention set that they are familiar with or prefer due to their expertise, instead of selecting an intervention set that uniquely addresses the performance problems of the client. Consultants should look at each intervention in the set as having a unique power to assist in reducing the performance gap.*

A cookie cutter approach is a figurative phrase meaning to think myopically, or to stay within the box, using a one size fits all or a standard intervention to address all performance problems. Although a cookie cutter approach may make it easy for the consultant to implement, it goes against the reality of addressing performance problems in dynamic organizations. While expertise is important, a consultant should not make the mistake of solely using the interventions in which they have the most experience. Training as an intervention is commonly selected in performance improvement initiatives. At times training is the only intervention selected when a novice or an individual with no performance improvement knowledge or experience is managing the initiative. Training is not the only go-to intervention; consultants should be wary of overly implementing any familiar or signature intervention. For example, if a consultant is an expert in implementing incentive programs, they might be tempted to often offer an incentive program as an intervention to their clients. In some cases, a consultant may be sought out by a client based on their expertise in a particular intervention. As a result, the client may expect that intervention to be chosen in the final intervention set. Despite client expectations, however, the essence of an intervention set should not allow for a cookie-cutter intervention set but instead the consultant should tailor the intervention set based on the performance problem. By using the enforcement schema, a consultant is able to quickly expand their thinking about what other interventions could reinforce other more foundational interventions in the set to enable equilibrium. The consultant should always think about the multiple forces working in an intervention set situation. Since every situation will consist of multiple diverse forces arranged in any number of different ways, a consultant should not take a cookie-cutter approach to intervention set selection.

Permeating Principle 4: Intervention set modelling (ISM)

> *Intervention Set Modelling (ISM). ISM is a prerequisite to prototyping and iteration because it serves a practical method to enable strategic thinking. It allows for a simple modeling technique and should be used as a way to identify connections and gaps among and between the interventions in the set from a macro level.*

The 4th permeating principle, intervention set modeling a prerequisite to prototyping and iteration, builds on Wedman and Tessmer's (1990) work on expert designers creating iterations of rapid prototyping as deliverables. As well as, Spitzer (1999) idea of an iterative approach. However, these authors do not offer any recommendations for strategically thinking about the rapid prototyping and iterative process before it is executed. In addition to creating rapid prototypes of individual interventions, consultants should use the intervention set modelling (ISM) technique to make rapid visual prototypes of the intervention sets, which in turn will stimulate the consultant's mechanism of action schemata making it easier to put the intervention set into practice at the prototyping stage. ISM is a simple modeling technique and should be used as a way to see connections and gaps among and between the interventions in the set from a macro level. The diagramming technique quickly communicates the interventions set to partners, collaborators, and the client for buy-in, resources, and additional time if needed. This method was inspired by the Socratic (469 – 399 BC) approach to teaching whereby mapping is used to understand a concept, its use, and its relationship to other items in the environment. This study presents the intervention set modeling (ISM) technique as a prerequisite to rapid prototyping and iteration.

When a consultant retrieves the mechanism of action schema, they are relying on past experience and research to justify the necessity of a particular intervention. However, there is also a creative element involved in the selection process. A consultant may look at the intervention set and see, based on experience, that there is an imbalance in the set. Intervention set modeling is also a useful tool for a consultant because it provides a visual representation of the set and enables them and others to reflect on the gaps in their intuitive reasoning. Consultants' experiences allow them to trust their intuition more than a novice might if placed in the same situation lacking analysis.

Consultants frequently encounter the human tendency to deny evidence that is not appealing.

Performance improvement authors suggest that it is the interpretation of data that allows the consultant to connect the dots between multiple interventions to address performance problems; this is the art or craft elements of the profession (Dessinger, Moseley, and Van Tiem, 2012; Robinson and Robinson, 2006). This text argues that the artistic element of performance improvement can go beyond the analysis phase and is a part of the intervention set selection phase as well. The idea that an intervention set is aesthetically pleasing or has some artistic elements means that the consultant adheres to the principles outlined in this book governing intervention set selection. It also means that the intervention set becomes well ingrained into the organization and evolves into a standard operating procedure.

Permeating Principle 5: Be open to continuous feedback

Be open to continuous feedback. A consultant should always listen to all feedback about an intervention set. This allows the consultant to use others as sounding boards for what will and what will not work. Too often consultants only attempt to gain buy-in at the beginning of a project and assume the buy-in will be sustained throughout the performance improvement process. The consultant must think about when they are no longer a part of the initiative, so they should listen and be aware of critics and take notes regarding potential flaws.

A continuous feedback loop can take a variety of forms from surveys and instructor evaluations, to instructional performance testing, to participate performance, to return on investment analysis. The hallmark of a successful performance improvement initiative is that it is self-sustaining and allows the client to make appropriate adjustments as needed without total dependence on a consultant.

INTERVENTION SET SELECTION SUBSTANTIVE THEORY

A substantive theory of intervention set selection below presents three distinct components of the theory of intervention set selection:

1. Comprehending the situation as it relates to the client, the analysis, the problem, and the literature

2. Activating schemata to synthesize an intervention set

3. Adhering to principles

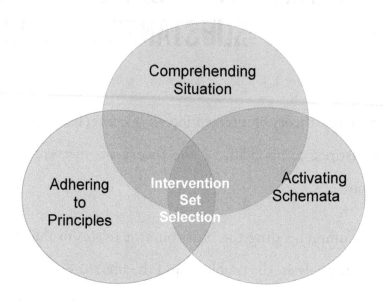

Figure 7: Intervention Set Selection Substantive Theory

Figure 7. Intervention Set Selection Substantive Theory. This figure illustrates how three components of selection work as one to generate intervention set selection.

Component 1: Comprehension of the situation

There is no denying the significance of continuously analyzing the situation and context in which the performance problem rests. The need for a consultant to understand their client, analysis, problem, and literature is seen as the first step towards the selection of an intervention. The notion of understanding the situation is briefly mentioned in the literature by Dean Spitzer (Stolovitch & Keeps, 1992). Comprehending the situation is traditionally viewed within the analysis domain of the performance improvement discipline; however, as Allison Rossett notes analysis should be emphasized as much or more in the intervention planning and execution stage (Stolovitch & Keeps, 1992). The consultant is always thinking of the client, results of the analysis, problem, and where it all fits into the literature. It is in this component that the consultant is setting the stage for the activation of schemata to synthesize the intervention set.

Behaviors demonstrating component 1 include:

- determining how the client self-diagnosed problem
- determining what home remedies client implemented
- conducting an analysis

- analyzing the performance data
- recalling performance improvement literature and research to place situation into context
- identify what other interventions could be connected to the interventions that emerged as a result of the analysis

Component 2: Activating schemata

After comprehending the situation, the consultant activates schemata. Schemata can be activated at any time during the intervention selection process. The data that are generated about the client, analysis, problem, and the literature are used to fuel the processing mechanism that activates the schemata. Comprehending the situation helps the consultant to make deliberate choices about what to do with the incoming data. Schemata are not static but constantly changing and as new data comes into view throughout the performance improvement process schemata evolve.

This component in the theory of intervention set selection is known as activating schemata to synthesize an intervention set and is where the constant iteration of design and development takes place. It is also where diagramming and rapid prototyping takes places to illustrate the intervention sets and connections to sub-sets. As the consultant expands in experiencing performance improvement problems, repertoire of schemata to retrieve will grow through what Mandler (1984) refers to as accommodation and assimilation. Schemata accommodation and assimilation allows the consultant to address more complex performance problems because of capacity to retrieve more complex schemata embedded in abstract schema are now more available in stored memory (Mandler, 1984, p. 62-63). The schemata that support substantive theory of intervention set selection are provided below.

The first schemata that are activated are referred to as the *composition schemata*. Composition schemata aid the consultant in making a simple yet critical decision in the intervention set selection process, that is, select a single intervention or a set of interventions. As noted, it is rare to have a single intervention as the only intervention needed to address a performance problem; however, it is the initial mistake novice or unskilled consultants make when in the intervention selection phase of the performance improvement process. *Directional schemata* guide the consultant as they explore the depth and breadth needed for each linkage in the intervention set. The dimensional set schema help the consultant examine an intervention set's depth under a particular performance factor. While the linear set schema guides the consultant cross the span of all performance factors. The consultant must be mindful of possible gaps in the results of an analysis. The *mechanism of action schemata* helps the consultant to see what additional interventions need to be activated in order for interventions that were identified via the analysis to be properly implemented. The intervention that serves as the mechanism of action can be located anywhere in a set and active another intervention vertically, horizontally, or a combination of both. The *enforcement schemata* helps the consultant decide if an intervention needs to be reinforced by another intervention. These schemata are important because they provide the consultant with checkpoint opportunities to see if identified interventions are stable enough on their own or require enforcement. When selecting an intervention set a consultant must consider the consequences or impact of each intervention selected within the set. The *transformation schemata* enables the consultant to consider the impact or transformation power each intervention has on one another or on the set as a whole. *Reverberation schemata* provide the consultant with a quick way to think about how the intervention set as a whole will impact the organization. These schemata are critical to the intervention set selection process because an intervention set can intentionally or unintentionally cause a distribution in other parts of the organization.

Component 3: Adhere to principles

Adhering to principles is the foundational behavior associated with the process of intervention set selection. Adherences to these principles complement the schemata developed. The schemata presented here provide a way for consultants to think about intervention set selection, while the principles provide a way to for the schemata to evolve throughout the selection process. See *APPENDIX A. Intervention Set Selection Job Aid* for the Intervention Set Selection Principles.

CHAPTER 6

CONCLUSION

Scholars have not provided the field with adequate direction on how the process occurs, specifically guidance on how practitioners bridge the intervention selection phase with the analysis phase. The analysis and design literature also did not provide adequate insight as to how to select intervention sets. As a result, what is known about intervention selection is limited. By focusing on the topic here, this book demonstrates how the inclusion of an intervention set selection phase in the performance improvement process can address these knowledge gaps as well as expand the knowledge base of performance improvement.

This text provides a substantive theory for interventions set selection and begins to explain the correlation between a consultant's comprehension of the performance situation in the context of client, analysis, the problem, and the literature, the activation of schemata, and the adherence of principles. The substantive theory of interventions set selection meets the criteria set forth by Glaser and Strauss (1967) for judging a substantive theory which are: fit, understandability, generalizability, and control.

The substantive theory of intervention set selection meets the criterion of fit because it is a practical and functional idea that can be applied by novice and skilled consultants. The theory is a simplistic three phase theory that can be understood by consultants who are not performance improvement professionals but have an interest in intervention set selection. The theory is generalizable in the sense that it can be applied to a multitude of industries and a wide range of performance improvement situations. The intervention set selection theory provides the consultant with control by relaying on fundamental schemata and principles. Future research needs to be focused on formalizing the theory.

This text only scratches the surface of research possibilities on the topic of intervention set selection. This chapter summarizes the key lessons of the study and implications. It concludes with a caution against maintaining the status quo of practice, teaching, and research in the area of intervention set selection.

Lesson 1 – Practitioners select intervention sets

The book focuses on building knowledge around how practicing professionals select interventions. As explained, there is little evidence to suggest only one intervention being selected to address a performance gap, which demonstrated that interventions were selected in the form of a set and not as a singular entity. For example, even if the intervention selected was training, there was another intervention selected that supported the training. Supporting interventions within the set may include goals, policies, procedures, or even job aids. This resulted in the creation and defining of the term *intervention set selection*. The establishment of the term intervention set selection and its meaning has significance for both the practice and the research of performance improvement. Incorporating a more accurate term such as intervention set selection may seem like a subtle contribution to the discipline, but it does have an influence on the behavior of practitioners and researchers. Expanding the terminology to include intervention set selection enables scholars to rethink the phenomenon of intervention selection, thus opening the possibility for more targeted studies on sets of interventions. Additionally, which terminology is used and how it is used is important for communication within and outside of the field. Accuracy in terminology enables practitioners to be more precise about what they deliver and increases the impact they have on organizations.

Practitioners' use of schemata was the second part of the answer to the question of how professionals select interventions. In addition to the art and intuition elements of intervention set selection, a practitioner's use of schemata illustrates that intervention set selection is a skill that can be developed. As an individual is exposed to more performance improvement experiences, their knowledge of schemata expands, and practitioners' ability to act on schemata becomes more of an automatic behavior. Likewise, schemata help scholars to better understand how expert practitioners are able to streamline problem solving and make connections in a situation where analysis is limited.

Lesson 2 – There are discernable patterns

Throughout the original study, patterns were observed in the data. One emergent pattern was the form of guiding principles practitioners followed when conducting intervention set selection. The second type of observed pattern involved various characteristics of the schemata found. See *APPENDIX A. Intervention Set Selection Job Aid* for a visual representation of intervention set selection schemata. One of the goals of scientific inquiry is to develop predictions and generalizations to explain phenomena. By identifying these discernable patterns, this book sets the foundation for generalization about intervention set selection and initial prediction studies on intervention sets.

Lesson 3 – There are guiding principles

Principles serve as guides that define how to select an intervention set, explain "how" and "why" certain actions happen during the intervention set selection phase, and function as a guide for novice and expert practitioners when selecting intervention sets in a variety of unique situations. As much as possible, expert practitioner's experiences with using principles in real-world contexts should be documented in case studies. This will enable students of performance improvement to learn from the experiences of others and inspire future research so the field's knowledge base can be expanded.

Lesson 4 – Intervention set schemata exist

There are schematic elements involved in the intervention set selection process. The development of *composition, directional dependence, mechanism of action, enforcement, transformation,* and *reverberation* schemata adds new knowledge to the field of performance improvement. The identification of these schemata help to explain a practitioner's systematic behaviors when selecting an intervention set. Schemata also help to illustrate the art and the science inherent in intervention set selection.

Depending on how a practitioner uses them, schemata may help or hinder innovation in intervention set selection. Therefore, it is necessary to provide the risks and concerns associated with these findings. The first concern, as alluded above, is the possibility that schemata can stifle innovation if used incorrectly. Practitioners should not simply use these schemata as procedural guidelines for how to select an intervention, but instead they should view these schemata as foundational reference points for starting the intervention set selection phase of the performance improvement process. Keeping an open mind, absorbing new research, and embracing different perspectives are essential. In turn, the art and intuition principles are also important to the process and complement the schemata. The principles that evolved help to mitigate the risk of practitioners stifling innovation as a result of using particular schemata. The schemata presented are suggested for novice consultants and students seeking knowledge on how to refine their intervention set selection skills. It is also intended to serve as a spark of inspiration for future researchers to further test and formalize the ideas informing the substantive theory of intervention set selection. A job aid is provided to assist readers in their application of the intervention set selection substantive theory. See *APPENDIX* A. *Intervention Set Selection Job Aid* for a quick reference guide on how to engage in the intervention set selection process using the components of the substantive theory provided.

Lesson 5 – Substantive theory of intervention set selection

In the introduction of this book, it was asked: Is there an underlying theory or model that can be developed that explains intervention selection, including specific relationships between performance factors? If so, what is the theory and does it inform intervention selection? This book presents the substantive theory of intervention set selection. The generated schemata provided the foundation for the types of relationships that exist between performance factors. By identifying the actions involved in the intervention set selection process, the substantive theory of intervention set selection enhances the understanding of the performance improvement selection process

Future endeavors

To further solidify the substantive theory of intervention set selection, this work suggests the following research and scholarly endeavors.

1. An Intervention Set Selection Textbook

An intervention set selection textbook would provide scholars and practitioners, at various experience levels, with core knowledge, research, real world case studies, and best practices associated with intervention set selection. The textbook could also serve as a main source or hub for finding information about particular interventions or even serve as an encyclopedia or library for interventions sets.

2. New Case Studies

The basic components of the intervention set selection substantive theory can be examined by using a new set of case studies. For example, by using new cases a researcher can characterize the interventions sets in each case against the schemata presented in the original dissertation to investigate whether they fall into one or more of the schemata. The researcher can also examine whether or not the consultants in the case abided the principles outlined in this study.

3. Measuring Comprehensiveness and Longevity

An objective of the intervention set selection process is to select an intervention set that is sufficiently comprehensive enough to reduce a performance gap. A future study could and should measure the correlation between an interventions set's comprehensiveness and a consultant's exposure to the theory, schemata, and principles in this study. Before this could be done, however, scholars would need to develop measurements and standards to assess the comprehensiveness of an intervention set. A future study could also examine whether the comprehensiveness and longevity of an intervention set differs by industry; for example, intervention sets within the information technology industry may differ from those in the agricultural industry or the healthcare industry.

4. Expert and Client Inquiry

To investigate the utility of the substantive theory of intervention set selection and its individual components, a researcher can survey or interview experienced consultants in field to see if the theory resonates with their practice. Similarly, a researcher can conduct a study that measures client satisfaction with both consultants who do and who do not abide by the principles offered by this study as well as those that engage their clients in intervention set selection modelling activities throughout their project.

5. Action Research in Educational Settings

Professors interested in performance improvement, specifically intervention set selection, can introduce the findings of the study to their students. While teaching, the professor can engage in action research techniques to examine student understanding of the theory's three components. For example, one of the obstacles a novice must learn to overcome when first exposed to the intervention selection process is thinking about interventions as a set rather than as a single entity. Using the schemata provided, a professor can more effectively increase students' ability to understand how to select more comprehensive intervention sets.

Reflections

This book confronts readers with ideas that will force the expansion of scholarly thinking in performance improvement. To truly move these findings from theory to meaningful human improvement contributions involves collective scholarly energy and individual commitment. The challenge for consultants and scholars now is to apply these findings to practice, teaching, and research. This requires the integration of schemata, principles, and the substantive theory of intervention set selection into ideas, terminology, practice, research, and teaching. Future decisions will rely more on data driven points of reference, and scholars must meet this challenge directly by producing research. While adopting intervention set selection is essential for the advancement of human performance, it is also necessary for the reduction of persistent human problems that are detrimental to organizational and societal improvements. In daily life one can see skill and knowledge interventions being presented as the main, if not the only, interventions for addressing issues such as gender inequality, environmental pollution, generational poverty, and correctional institution recidivism. Human performance problems are becoming more complex and the interventions sets needed to address them will require depth, breadth, and impact with higher return rates. Solely relying on skill and knowledge interventions as a planned panaceas for addressing human performance problems is no longer sufficient and to some extent negligent. Such myopic thinking impedes innovation. The author urges individuals in academia, business, government, and the nonprofit sector to adopt this approach to intervention set selection and build upon its principles and schemata to improve the future for all humanity.

REFERENCES

Bertalanffy, L. (1972). The history and status of general systems theory. Academy of Management Journal, 15(4), 407-426.

Brethower, D. (1999). General systems theory and behavioral psychology. In H. Stolovitch & E. Keeps (Eds.), Handbook of human performance technology: Improving individual and organizational performance worldwide (pp. 67-81). San Francisco, CA: Jossey-Bass-Pfeiffer.

Chyung, S. (2005). Human performance technology from Taylor's scientific management to Gilbert's behavior engineering model. *Performance Improvement*, 44(1), 23- 28.

Clark, R., & Estes, F. (2000). A proposal for the collaborative development of authentic performance technology. *Performance Improvement, 39*(4), 48-53.

Dessinger, J., Moseley, J., & Tiem, D. (2012). Performance improvement/HPT model: Guiding the process. *Performance Improvement, 51*(3), 10-17.

Dictionary.com. Set. Retrieved November 11, 2014, from http://dictionary.reference.com/browse/set?s=t

Gilbert, T. (1978). *Human competence: Engineering worthy performance.* New York, NY: McGraw-Hill.

Gilbert, T. (2007). *Human competence: Engineering worthy performance* (Tribute ed.). San Francisco, CA: Pfeiffer.

Gilmore, E. (2009). *An evaluation of the efficacy of Wile's taxonomy of human performance factors.* Bloomington: Indiana University.

Girard, M., Lapides, J., & Roe, C. (2006). The fifth discipline: A systems learning model for building high-performing learning organizations. In J. Pershing (Ed.), *Handbook of human performance technology: Principles, practice, potential* (3rd ed., pp. 592-618). San Francisco, CA: Pfeiffer.

Gladwell, M. (2011). *Outliers: The story of success.* New York: Back Bay Books.

Glaser, B., & Strauss, A. (1967). *The discovery of grounded theory: Strategies for qualitative research.* Chicago, IL: Aldine.

Langdon, D., Whiteside, K., & McKenna, M. (1999). *Intervention resource guide: 50 performance improvement tools*. San Francisco, CA: Jossey-Bass/Pfeiffer.

Mandler, G. (1984). *Mind and body: Psychology of emotion and stress*. New York, NY: W.W. Norton.

Pershing, J. (2006). *Handbook of human performance technology: Principles, practices, and potential* (3rd ed.). San Francisco, CA: Pfeiffer.

Robinson, D., & Robinson, J. (2006). Making the transition from a learning to a performance function. In J. Pershing (Ed.), *Handbook of human performance technology: Principles, practice, potential* (3rd ed., pp. 903-923). San Francisco, CA: Pfeiffer.

Rosenberg, M. (1999). The general process of human performance technology. In H. Stolovitch & E. Keeps (Eds.), *Handbook of human performance technology: Improving individual and organizational performance worldwide* (pp. 137-138). San Francisco, CA: Jossey-Bass.

Rossett, A. (1992). Analysis of human performance problems. In H. Stolovitch & E. Keeps (Eds.), *Handbook of human performance technology: A comprehensive guide for analyzing and solving performance problem in organizations* (pp. 97113). San Francisco, CA: Jossey-Bass.

Rush, A. (2012). Client partnership throughout the performance improvement/human performance technology model. *Performance Improvement, 51*(9), 29-37.

Spitzer, D. (1992). The design and development of effective interventions. In H. Stolovitch & E. Keeps (Eds.), *Handbook of human performance technology: A comprehensive guide for analyzing and solving performance problem in organizations* (1st ed., pp. 114-129). San Francisco, CA: Jossey-Bass.

Spitzer, D. R. (1999). The design and development of effective interventions. In H.D. Stolovitch & E.J. Keeps (Eds.) Handbook of human performance technology: Improving individual and organizational performance worldwide (2nd ed.). (pp.163-184) San Francisco: Pfeiffer/ISPI.

Stolovitch, H. (2000). Human performance technology: Research and theory to practice. *Performance Improvement, 39*(4), 7-16.

Stolovitch, H., & Keeps, E. (1992). What is performance technology? In H. Stolovitch & E. Keeps (Eds.), *Handbook of human performance technology: A comprehensive guide for analyzing and solving performance problems in organizations* (pp. 3-13). San Francisco, CA: Jossey-Bass.

Stolovitch, H., & Keeps, E. (2006). Forward to Third Edition. In J. Pershing (Ed.), *Handbook of human performance technology: Principles, practice, potential* (3rd ed., pp. xii-xix). San Francisco, CA: Pfeiffer.

Stolovitch, H., & Keeps, E. (1992). *Handbook of human performance technology: A comprehensive guide for analyzing and solving performance problems in organizations.* San Francisco: Jossey-Bass.

Stolovitch, H., & Keeps, E. (2006). *Beyond training ain't performance fieldbook: Strategies, tools, and guidance for effective workplace performance.* Alexandria, VA: ASTD Press.

Symonette, S. G. (2015). *Developing principles and schemata for intervention set selection in human performance technology* (Doctoral dissertation, Indiana University).

Van Tiem, D., Moseley, J., & Dessinger, J. (2004). *Fundamentals of performance improvement: A guide to improving people, process, and performance.* (2nd ed.). Silver Spring, MD: International Society for Performance Improvement.

Wedman, J., & Tessmer, M. (1990). The "layers of necessity" ID model. *Performance Instruction, 29*(4), 1-7.

Wile, D. (1996). Why doers do. *Performance Instruction, 35*(2), 30-35.

APPENDIX A: INTERVENTION SET SELECTION JOB AID

Purpose of the Intervention Set Selection Job Aid
The intervention set selection job aid presents the three components of the intervention set selection substantive theory: Components: 1. Comprehending the situation as it relates to the client, the analysis, the problem, and the literature 2. Activating schemata to synthesize an intervention set 3. Adhering to principles In addition, this job aid summarizes the principles and schemata that support the execution of the intervention set selection process in practice. It serves as a quick reference guide to use when teaching, studying, and practicing intervention set selection. Educators, practitioners, and scholars are encouraged to use the job aid to think through each component of the intervention set selection process. Instead of skimming over the "how" and "why" of intervention set selection in the leap from the analysis phase to the design phase, the job aid helps the user to focus on the key components of intervention set selection. The ultimate goal of the job aid is to help the consultant better communicate the intervention set selection process to their clients and further articulate the value of their work through the process of intervention set selection.

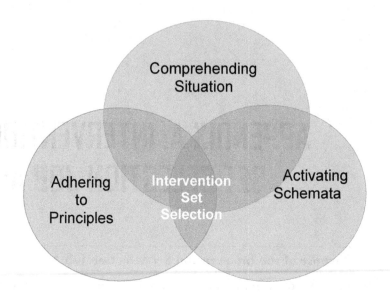

Figure 1: Intervention Set Selection Substantive Theory

Figure 1. Intervention Set Selection Substantive Theory. This figure illustrates how three components of selection work as one to generate intervention set selection

Component 1: Comprehension of the Situation
A consultant should always be thinking of the client, results of the analysis, problems, and where it all fits into the literature base. This is seen as the first step towards the selection of an intervention set. This component sets the stage for the activation of schemata that help in synthesizing the intervention set. Behaviors demonstrating comprehension of the situation include: ❑ Determining how the client self-diagnosed the problem ❑ Determining what home remedies the client is proposing ❑ Conducting an analysis ❑ Analyzing the performance data ❑ Recalling performance improvement literature and research to place situation into context ❑ Identify what other interventions could be connected to the interventions that were the result of the analysis

Component 2: Activating Schemata to Synthesize an Intervention Set

Schemata can be activated by the consultant at any time during the intervention selection process. This component is where the constant iteration of design and development takes place. It is also where diagramming and rapid prototyping are used to illustrate the intervention sets and their connections to sub-sets. As the consultant expands their experiences of performance improvement problems, their repertoire of retrievable schemata will grow. Schemata accommodation and assimilation allows the consultant to address more complex performance problems. The schemata that support the process of intervention set selection are listed below and are activated in combination with principles:

❏	Composition Schemata	❏	Enforcement Schemata
❏	Directional Dependence Schemata	❏	Transformation Schemata
❏	Mechanism of Action Schemata	❏	Reverberation Schemata

Component 3: Adhere to Principles

Schemata provide a way for consultants to think about intervention set selection, while the principles provide a way to manifest the schemata in the selection process. Intervention set selection principles are as followed:

❏ Prerequisite principles
❏ Initiating intervention set selection principles
❏ Permeating intervention set selection schemata principles

Prerequisite Principles
Prerequisite Principle 1. Novice consultants should begin by practicing on small performance improvement projects and by reading the work of more seasoned professionals in order to start acquiring foundational schemata. The combination of education and real world practice can vary; however, the goal is for the consultant to be well grounded in both applied research and practice. After a consultant has many years of experience and an advance degree in performance improvement, they must stay abreast of new research and additions to best practices as well as actively engage in professional associations. This is important so that experienced individuals do not become stuck in the habit of operating without incorporating new and improved methods, which in turn can render their practice stagnant.
Prerequisite Principle 2. A performance consultant must acquire expertise in all phases of the performance improvement process and have deep expertise in a particular industry or culture as well as a few interventions they have mastered. The consultant should be honest with themselves and the client about their skill level. When the consultant lacks needed expertise they should collaborate with an expert to supplement the lacking skill required for the intervention set to be executed in the organization.

Initiating Intervention Set Selection Principles
Initiating Principle 1: A performance consultant should demonstrate how the performance problem aligns with strategic goals. Establishing a connection between strategic goals and performance problems provides the consultant with an opportunity to gain and maintain the client's attention throughout the life of the project and builds creditability.

Initiating Principle 2: A performance consultant should inquire about any prior self-diagnosis activity conducted by the client to address the performance problem. In addition to analyzing the performance problem be ready to evaluate any home remedies initiated by the client.

Initiating Principle 3: A consultant must appropriately and wisely balance the use of data resulting from analysis and tacit knowledge as they navigate the intervention set selection phase of the performance improvement process. The two types of knowledge should not be viewed as dichotomies, but as counterparts working together to energize the intervention set selection phase.

Initiating Principle 4a: A consultant should act as an orchestra leader. To do this the consultant must be interconnected to people, networks, and ideas within and outside of the client organization. Consultant interconnectedness goes beyond general knowledge and awareness of these entities. Consultants should immerse themselves into these environments in order to assure that the selected intervention set ultimately fits into the current and evolving new environment. If the consultant is not interconnected they can potentially select an intervention set that quickly becomes obsolete because it does not fit within the environment.

Initiating Principle 4b: A consultant must work across disciplines, departments, and industries to select an intervention set that is comprehensive. Cross-functionality allows an intervention set to generate support and buy-in utilizing the knowledge base from other disciplines so that the set gains traction within the organization. Cross-functionality means more than just having the right people in the room and a diverse set of ideas on the table. It involves a deeper understanding of how cross-functional intervention sets impact performance. It requires conscious and deliberate connections between ideas and people. The consultant should be viewed as a creditable connector and selector of intervention sets that need to be implemented.

Permeating Intervention Set Selection Schemata Principles

Permeating ISS Schemata Principle 1a. A systems mindset needs to permeate the intervention set selection process. The consultant should pay special attention on what binds each intervention together as a set, how the complete set works together as one unified set, and how the set functions within an organization. A systems mindset during the intervention set selection process allows the analysis to be optimized through the use of the following schemata.

- ☐ Composition Schemata
- ☐ Directional Dependence Schemata
- ☐ Mechanism of Action Schemata
- ☐ Enforcement Schemata
- ☐ Transformation Schemata
- ☐ Reverberation Schemata

Permeating ISS Schemata Principle 1b. Consultants should always consider the consequences of each intervention selected as a part of an intervention set. In doing so, the consultant should look at all the interventions in the set as a whole to identify how they work together and what keeps them functioning cohesively. A consultant may not know all the consequences of the set with certainty, but a concerted effort should be taken to gain knowledge about potential risks.

Permeating ISS Schemata Principle 1c. It is the responsibility of the performance consultant to inform the client of the intentional or unintentional impact the selected intervention set may have on other parts of the organization and surrounding community.

Permeating ISS Schemata Principle 2. A consultant must move beyond only gathering evidence during the needs analysis phase and gather evidence on individual interventions and sets of interventions. This evidence should be sought through a deep understanding of performance improvement published research and theory as well as through evidence acquired during practical experience and observation in the field.

Permeating ISS Schemata Principle 3a. A consultant's intuition and artistic expression should not be ignored in the quest for scientific reasoning nor should it be the sole basis for the selection of an intervention set. Intuition and artistic expression need to be done in tandem within a scientific process and grounded in evidence-based practices.

Permeating ISS Schemata Principle 3b. Avoid the cookie cutter approach. A cookie cutter approach is a figurative phrase meaning to think myopically, or to stay within the box, using a one size fits all or a standard intervention to address all performance problems. It occurs when a consultant promotes an intervention set that they are familiar with or prefer due to their expertise, instead of selecting an intervention set that uniquely addresses the performance problems of the client. Consultants should look at each intervention in the set as having a unique power to assist in reducing the performance gap.

Permeating ISS Schemata Principle 4. Intervention set modeling (ISM) is a prerequisite to prototyping and iteration because it serves a practical method to enable strategic thinking. It allows for simple modeling technique and should be used as a way to see connections and gaps among and between the interventions in the set from a macro level.

Permeating ISS Schemata Principle 5. A consultant should always listen to all feedback about an intervention set. This allows the consultant to use others as sounding boards for what will and what will not work. Too often consultants only attempt to gain buy-in at the beginning of a project and assume that the buy-in will be sustained throughout the performance improvement process. The consultant must think about when they are no longer a part of the initiative, so they should listen and be aware of critics and take notes regarding potential flaws.

Composition schemata

The first schemata that are activated are referred to as the *composition schemata*. Composition schemata aid the consultant in making a simple and yet critical decision in the intervention set selection process: that is, select a single intervention or a set of interventions. As noted, it is rare to have a single intervention as the only intervention needed to address a performance problem; however, it is an initial mistake novice or unskilled consultants make when in the intervention selection phase of the performance improvement process.

Single Intervention	Intervention Set

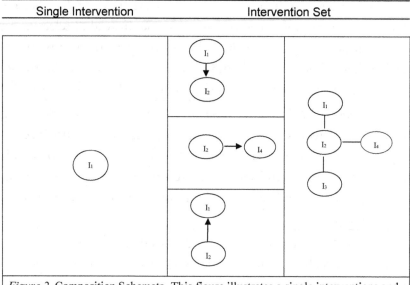

Figure 2. Composition Schemata. This figure illustrates a single interventions and intervention sets. I_1 Intervention 1. I_2 Intervention 2. I_3 Intervention 3. I_4 Intervention 4

Figure 2: Composition Schemata

Directional Schemata

Directional schemata guide the consultant as they explore the depth and breadth needed for each linkage in the intervention set. The dimensional set schema helps the consultant examine an intervention set's depth under a particular performance factor. While the linear set schema guides the consultant cross the span of all performance factors.

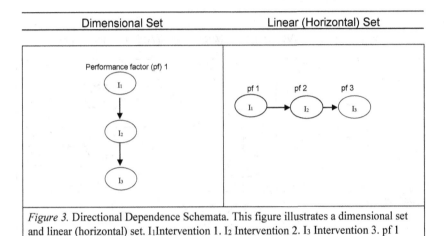

Figure 3. Directional Dependence Schemata. This figure illustrates a dimensional set and linear (horizontal) set. I_1 Intervention 1. I_2 Intervention 2. I_3 Intervention 3. pf 1 Performance factor 1. pf 2 Performance factor 2. pf 3 Performance factor 3.

Figure 3: Directional Dependence Schema

Mechanism of action schemata

The consultant must be mindful of possible gaps in the results of an analysis. The *mechanism of action schemata* helps the consultant to see what additional interventions need to be activated in order for interventions that were the result of the analysis to be properly implemented. The intervention that serves as the mechanism of action can be located anywhere in a set and activate another intervention vertically, horizontally, or a combination of both.

Mechanism of Action 1 (Vertical)   Mechanism of Action II (Horizontal)

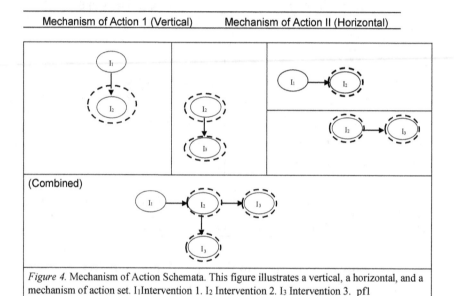

Figure 4. Mechanism of Action Schemata. This figure illustrates a vertical, a horizontal, and a mechanism of action set. I₁Intervention 1. I₂ Intervention 2. I₃ Intervention 3. pf1 Performance factor 1. ❨❩ Mechanism that activates a connection between another intervention

Figure 4: Mechanism of Action Schemata

Enforcement Schemata
The *enforcement schemata* helps the consultant decide if an intervention needs to be reinforced by another intervention. These schemata are important because they provide the consultant with checkpoint opportunities to see if the identified interventions are stable enough on their own or require enforcement. When selecting an intervention set a consultant must consider the consequences or impact of each intervention selected within the set.

One-way Enforcement Set	Two-way Enforcement Set

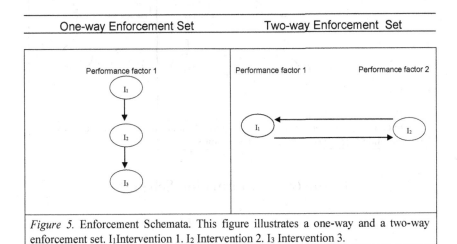

Figure 5. Enforcement Schemata. This figure illustrates a one-way and a two-way enforcement set. I_1 Intervention 1. I_2 Intervention 2. I_3 Intervention 3.

Figure 5: Enforcement Schemata

Transformation Schemata

The *transformation schemata* enables the consultant to consider the impact or transformation power each intervention has on one another or the set as a whole.

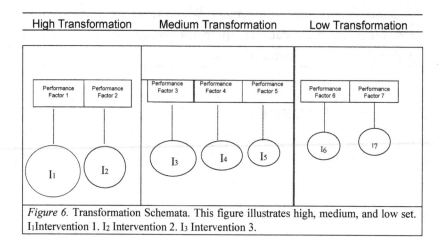

High Transformation   Medium Transformation   Low Transformation

Figure 6. Transformation Schemata. This figure illustrates high, medium, and low set. I_1 Intervention 1. I_2 Intervention 2. I_3 Intervention 3.

Figure 6: Transformation Schemata

Reverberation Schemata

Reverberation schemata provide the consultant with a quick way to think about how the intervention set as whole will impact the organization. These schemata are critical to the intervention set selection process because an intervention set can intentionally or unintentionally cause distributions in other parts of the organization.

Narrow Reverberation	Wide Reverberation

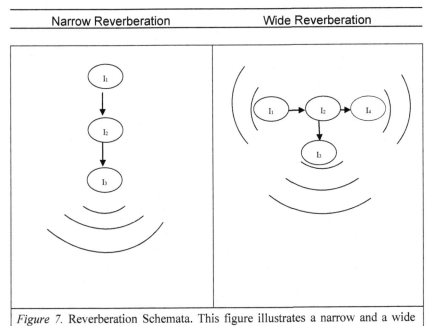

Figure 7. Reverberation Schemata. This figure illustrates a narrow and a wide reverberation set. I_1Intervention 1. I_2 Intervention 2. I_3 Intervention 3.

Figure 7: Reverberation Schemata

Printed in the United States
by Baker & Taylor Publisher Services